Evolve yourself

conscious personal evolution

Rich Rahn

a Duh! book

Like this book? Want to use part of it for something?
You'll need written permission. Duh!
Contact Duh! Books at *duhbooks@yahoo.com*.

Evolve yourself: conscious personal evolution / Rich Rahn
ISBN 0-9665593-04
1. Conscious Evolution. 2. Personal Evolution.
3. Self Help. 4. Psychology/Philosophy.

Duh! Books
1660 Bloomfield Place Drive, Suite 309C
Bloomfield Hills, MI 48302
duhbooks@yahoo.com

Cover design by John Ozdych
© Copyright 1998 **Duh! Books**
Back cover photo: Rich Rahn age 5

Edited by Mary O'Neill

Special thanks to Lorraine Brogan and L.G.R.

Thanks Mary

Contents

Evolve Yourself

Introdu*h*ction

"In the middle of the way of our lives,
I found myself in a dark, dangerous wood."
– Dante

"Feed your head."
– Jefferson Airplane

They say you learn one way or the other. For most of my life I learned the "other."

Then one day, it occurred to me I wasn't going to die young and I started having some real questions about the meaning of life. About what it is and how it works. But I wasn't satisfied with the answers I was getting. It slowly dawned on me I didn't know anything about what really mattered. All the standard explanations didn't ring true or even begin to help me get any satisfaction out of life. Little

Evolve Yourself

did I know I was entering Dante's dark wood, the beginning of the soul's high adventure.

In the course of my searching, I realized that everyone must address the question sooner or later in their own lives. You know, THE QUESTION. What is the meaning of life? Or more simply put, who am I? To some it's a little voice they do their best to ignore, a vague irritant. But to others it literally screams. Lucky me.

Even when everything appeared to be going well on the surface of my life, beneath it all a dark undertow of doubt and fear was pulling hard, sweeping the sand from beneath my feet. Something was wrong or missing or both. I had to admit it – I was lost (and you know how hard it is for a man to admit he's lost!) I instinctively knew I was living only a fraction of what life could be. Sound familiar? The trouble is that it's hard to see the whole picture when you're inside the frame.

What to do?

Well, I fought, thought and read a lot. I studied, pondered, experimented, failed, flailed, tried again, kept an open mind to life and found things which are helping me get in tune with the Big Mystery. To help answer THE QUESTION. You're welcome to use these ideas and hopefully benefit from them.

I've appropriated ideas from the best minds in history. From Jesus to Joseph Campbell, Aristotle to Ayn

Evolve Yourself

Rand, Henry Miller to Herculitus, Buddha to Bucky Fuller, from my Grandmother to my young son. I've synthesized something old, something new, something borrowed and something blue to better understand this intricate yet ultimately simple thing called life.

We're all going to need a clear vision of what it means to be human in order to thrive in this new millennium. So read this with fresh eyes, use an open mind, be honest and not too serious. And, always remember, you have to evolve. Yourself.

But first I want to share a story from my childhood which explains the "Duh!" theme running through this book and that also suggests in everyone's life there are experiences which, when looked at metaphorically, give us great insight into the mystery of life and sometimes unexpected wisdom. We've all had them. The trick is to recognize these experiences and learn from them.

duh (dŭh) *avd.* **1.** An expression uttered when something becomes obvious; Example: "Oh, I get it. duh!" **2.** The response to the realization that things aren't always self-evident, direct or straightforward. **3.** Articulated at understanding the paradoxical nature of truth. Example: "Now I *really* get it. Duh!"

Evolve Yourself

The Maze Story

"Until we lose ourselves, there is no hope of finding ourselves."
– Henry Miller

"Truth is that which works."
– Buddha

Nearly every summer when I was growing up, my mom, dad, older sister and I took off for a week or two long road adventure.

We'd see the USA in our Chevrolet (or Pontiac or Plymouth or whatever.) We'd camp along the way, sharing the same small, wonderfully smelly canvas tent. Our diet consisted mostly of corn flakes, baloney sandwiches and macaroni and cheese. For a young boy, it was heaven.

Our mom initiated these trips. She pinched pennies

all winter and planned our itinerary. Mom was a teacher at heart so our trips always had "themes." They may have been educational, but they were never dull.

One year, we covered the "Lincoln Trail," driving to every historical site involving our 16th President that time and distance would allow. We saw the log cabin where Abe was born. (I imagined him splitting rails and reading by firelight.) We followed his path to the state legislature in Springfield, Illinois and then to Washington, D.C., culminating in a tour of our nation's capitol.

Along the way, we stopped at Civil War battlefields or anywhere else that was of interest from Grandma Moses' house to a button museum.

One year, we followed the Lewis and Clark trail all the way to the Pacific. In 1964, we visited the World's Fair in New York. By the time I was 10 or 11, I had been in each of the 48 contiguous states. (A fact I was not shy about sharing during the school year, causing a teacher to call my parents to see if I actually had been in every state or was just a liar.)

The summer I turned eight, our trip included a stop at a mansion that undoubtedly had historical significance. What or where it was, I honestly don't remember, but I'll never forget that day and what I learned there.

The place was immense, a huge estate with spacious, stately grounds. While Mom went inside to peruse the brochures and see about a guided tour, Dad took my

Evolve Yourself

sister and me to have a look around and "stretch our legs."

We walked to the back of the mansion and were instantly surrounded by beautiful formal gardens complete with a maze. Perfectly groomed tall hedges lined narrow sidewalks that led every which way, and ultimately to the center of the maze.

Determined to get to the center before my older sister and aching to show my dad just how smart I was, I rushed into the entrance.

I tore down those little sidewalks as only an eight-year-old boy can, around corners and down pathways until they dead-ended. I backtracked, tried different paths and took whatever turns presented themselves, determined to beat my sister to the center of the maze.

But to no avail. I found my way back to the entrance without any problem, I just couldn't get to the center. I looked through the thick hedges, called for my sister, turned left, turned right, double-backed. I tried just about everything I could think of without any luck. I was frustrated, hot, tired, thirsty, confused, a little scared and damned near tears.

Now, unbeknownst to me, my father had been watching the entire time from an observation deck on the back of the mansion. He had a complete view of the maze and saw me running around like a crazed lab rat. He watched me go in, get lost and come out a dozen times.

From his vantage point he could clearly see the way

Evolve Yourself

to the center. He relayed this information to my sister who, after what seemed like forever, found me, took me by the hand and led me back to the entrance. There, she proceeded to "show me the way" in that obnoxious, condescending manner that only big sisters have.

At the entrance we had a choice: we could turn either right or left. And there was a sign. I can still see it. A simple freestanding sign like the kind you see in a bank line or at a movie theater.

This sign had an arrow on it. No words. Just a little arrow pointing to the left. The unspoken message being "Go This Way… Go Left."

But my sister, with me in tow, turned right and before I could even fathom this blatant breech of the rules, we were in the center. The elusive center. Complete with drinking fountains, shade trees and people having a wonderful time.

I was dumbfounded. I was outraged, shocked and appalled. It didn't fit. It was wrong. I said to my sister "But you didn't go the right way!"

Her one word reply said it all, "Duh!"

That was all she said, but it spoke volumes. And still does. You hear it all the time from kids and grownups. Duh means "Tell me something I *don't* know." Duh means "Hello! Obvious!"

And, the subtext of "Duh" is that things aren't always self-evident, direct or straightforward, and that ulti-

Evolve Yourself

mately, truth is paradoxical. "Duh" means that sometimes you have to think about things differently.

I went back to the entrance of the maze and watched people enter and, unquestioning, turn left, following the silent command of the sign. The thought of going against the direction of the arrow was so foreign to me, it wouldn't have occurred to me to go the other way. I had been taught to follow the rules, not to question them. It had served me well thus far.

But not that day at the maze. I learned two things that day. First, like my father had on the observation deck, a view of the big picture is essential to finding your way. And secondly, if you want to get to the center, you have to realize that sometimes the arrows may be pointing the wrong way.

Evolve Yourself

Something is happening

"We are in the midst of a revelatory experience of the universe that must be compared in its magnitude with those of the great religious revelations. And we only need wander about telling this new story to ignite a transformation of humanity."
— B. Swimme
"For the times, they are a-changin'."
— Bob Dylan

Something is happening.

And, unless you're a disciple of biology, sociology, cosmology, theology, psychology, philosophy, anthropology, physics, metaphysics and quantum physics, you may not even know it.

What is it? What is "happening?"

New discoveries in all these fields of human knowledge are rapidly replacing our current understandings about life. Entrenched ideas that have dominated our cul-

Evolve Yourself

ture for hundreds of years are being blown away almost daily. And this new information is bringing about a different way of looking at the world. A fresh perspective.

Whether through science or religion, mankind has always searched for one thing. A unified theory. We're looking for the big explanation. The Answer. Something that connects; something that reconciles opposites and makes us whole. A single theme that harmonizes our inner selves with our outer world and gives meaning to our lives. We've searched for balance between our biological, physical selves and our spiritual, emotional selves.

Guess what? The answer is here. And the understanding of it is radically changing not only what we know, but also our thoughts on who we are and where we're going.

For the first time in our history, experts in all fields of knowledge agree on one thing: there's a recognizable pattern of development that applies to all levels of existence. A plan.

This discovery has motivated us to radically reassess how we view the world and this new perspective is leading us to the next level of human development. The experts are calling it our conscious evolution.

They say timing is everything. And what a perfect time to review, reflect and reevaluate. The New Millennium. Like New Year's Eve on steroids. Time to sit back and take

Evolve Yourself

a hard look at who we are, what we know and where we're going.

We've been moving toward our conscious evolution as individuals through the pursuit of personal growth, eclectic spirituality and healthier lifestyles; and as societies through advances in technology, medicine, mass communication and global politics.

Still, many of us cling to outdated world views and although we live in the Information Age, it's hard to replace that old, comfortable, it's-worked-for-me-so-far mindset.

Now, you can believe and participate in myth, religion, past life regression, psychotherapy, drugs, booze, whatever, but if you don't have a firm grasp of what's real, you'll never be truly happy. You'll have an unnamed internal conflict, which you'll blame on everything from the economy to your parents. Your life will continue to be out of balance to one degree or another as long as you shut your eyes to what's real.

The secret to a truly happy and fulfilled life has always been to create harmony between your inner reality and the outer reality of the world. To do this you have to first see and accept the truth about the outer world. As it is, as we know it, thus far.

There are new scientific discoveries about the nature of reality that you may or may not know about

Evolve Yourself

that will unquestionably have a profound influence on society and our personal lives. In one way or another, this new knowledge is going to change your life. Much in the same way life changed for people when they found out the world wasn't flat!

And one thing is for sure, the changes are already happening.

Evolve Yourself

The universe is alive

"The most important thing about a man is his view of the universe."
— G.K. Chesterton

"The universe is always expanding and expanding in every direction it can whiz…"
— Monty Python

Ancient civilizations and native peoples believed the universe was ruled by gods and goddesses. Angry gods, loving gods. Gods who ruled over love and beauty, peace and war, the oceans and the sun. At any moment a god could show his or her wrath or approval. The universe was viewed as a passionate, stimulating, magical place. And, in the absence of hard scientific data, the god-ruling universe was a theory that worked well. Man lived to please the gods and in turn was comforted as they believed each god did their part to keep the world in order.

*Our interpretation of the universe changes
with new information.*

*We now know the universe is not
like a mechanized clock.
It's constantly growing and expanding.*

Our view the universe is reflected in our lives.

But then a bunch of thinkers – Copernicus, Galileo, Newton – challenged the conventional wisdom with their discoveries and theories about the cosmos. It was a long struggle and many of these great thinkers were persecuted for their ideas, but eventually science prevailed over religion and mythology and a new view of how the universe operated took hold. The thinking was that the universe was like a big clock. A giant predictable machine, methodically cranking away keeping the proverbial ball of life rolling.

Then along came guys like Edwin Hubbell, Albert Einstein and Stephen Hawkings with discoveries indicating that the universe is not so mechanized or so lifeless. It's now widely accepted that the cosmos is constantly expanding, changing, growing and flourishing. Quasars, pulsars, stars being born and stars dying. Billions and billions of unimaginable thermonuclear explosions, galaxies upon galaxies, spinning into forever. We now see the universe as a dynamic, evolving, creative place. A magical place.

Consciously or unconsciously, our understanding of the universe affects every aspect of our lives. When the mechanistic worldview became the dominant metaphor for our culture, our social, political, educational and economic systems modeled and reflected the machine as the most efficient way of getting things done. Strictly adhered to routines and customs for living, working and loving emerged. Example: the Industrial Revolution, which cul-

Since we live what we know…

…and, what we know is changing…

…we are changing.

Evolve Yourself

minated with the assembly line, methodically cranked out everything from toasters to automobiles with clocklike precision.

With our new understanding of the universe as a dynamic, constantly changing entity, we're beginning to emerge, (refreshed, I believe) from that rigidity. Our institutions are becoming more organic and free-flowing, more creative and open to change.

Case in point: The World Wide Web. It's fast-growing, everywhere and nowhere at the same time. It's not mechanistic; it's lifelike. It grows and behaves like an organism, not a machine.

Another case in point: The family. The nuclear family consisting of a mother, father and their offspring is fast-receding into history. Step-moms, step-dads, half siblings, step-siblings, step-grandparents. Divorce, remarriage, gay families, biracial families, adoption, surrogate mothers, sperm donors. The family is evolving into ever greater complexity. Just like everything else.

Though we may never know the universe exactly as it is, our experience of it is reflected in our systems and in our cultural, political, social and personal lives. Because our experience of the universe is changing, it means, ultimately, we are changing, too.

Evolve Yourself

Everything is connected

"This we know: the earth does not belong to man; man belongs to the earth. This we know. All things are connected..."
— Chief Seattle

"We experience ourselves...
as something separate from the rest
— a kind of optical delusion."
— Albert Einstein

Science has recently verified what each of us instinctively know. Everything is connected.

We're familiar with the ecological connection story. How the delicate balance of an ecosystem can be violently tipped simply by wiping out the population of one animal, plant or insect. Because we are beginning to understand our connection to the earth, we now recycle, drive more fuel efficient vehicles, return our bottles, refrain from killing entire species and purchase products

---

We're not independent;
we're interdependent.

Everything affects everybody.

Science reveals everything is connected
by an intricate series of relationships...

...something we instinctively know...

made from recycled materials without even thinking twice about it.

We see how countries, economies, communications, events, politics and people are connected and interdependent. Political upheavals in one part of the world affect the economy in another part of the world. Medical advancements impact social agenda. Mass communication and travel, satellite technology, the Internet, fashion, food and entertainment trends know no borders. The media is like a great big planetary nervous system; something happens halfway around the world and we experience it immediately on CNN. The World Wide Web is the connecting "global brain."

Now a revelation comes to us from the study of quantum physics as to how penetrating and profound our connections truly are. Sub-atomic particles — the tiniest things known to man so far — are not "things" but rather connections between things. Instead of separate little "building blocks" making up our physical world, a "complex web of relationships " does. A complex web of relationships that connects all things; atoms, molecules, cells, organisms, plants, animals, people, countries, planets, galaxies all remarkably intertwined.

On a deep level, we instinctively know this. Why else, without even thinking about it, would a person risk their own life to save a stranger? According to Arthur

...we're all related.

Our separateness is an optical delusion.

Schopenhauer, such an act represents a metaphysical realization that you and the other are one. This is the teaching of all the great religious traditions. Love your neighbor as yourself. Love your neighbor because he is yourself. Because, ultimately that's how connected we are.

We may have a sense of separateness from the world around us. It's necessary in order for us to establish identity. But take it from Einstein, it just looks that way. Everything is connected.

Evolve Yourself

The evolution revolution

"Life did not take over the globe by combat,
but by networking."
— Lynn Margulis & Dorian Sagan

"The standard, glib, neo-Darwin explanation of natural selection
— absolutely nobody believes this anymore."
— Ken Wilber

Remember Darwin's Theory of Evolution? Forget it.

Well, okay, not entirely. But realize that Darwin's major conclusion — that all evolutionary progress results from random mutations followed by natural selection and survival of the fittest — is now viewed by the scientific community as fundamentally flawed. His assumption that the first appearance of life was a chance event led him to erroneously conclude that the environment had no interest whatsoever in sustaining it. He thought that if life were to

Evolution is not a theory or hypothesis. It's a fact.

The appearance of life was not accidental.
Life wants to happen.

Life transforms itself to higher levels by jumps or leaps,
not by a gradual "piling on" of mutations.

succeed at all, it faced a constant battle against a hostile environment. Darwin's thinking was mechanistic and reductionist – a product of his times.

Well, the times they are a-changin'

And our thinking is a-changin' with the times. We no longer think of evolution in terms of a "theory." It just is. Evolution *is*. It's at the heart of all things. Everything in the universe – including you – evolves. Evolution is the general condition. It's the one thing *everything* has in common. Period.

And we have a new understanding of *how* things evolve. For instance, Darwin thought that chance alone was responsible for the appearance of life in the universe. The truth is, when conditions are right, life emerges. Life wants to happen. It's not an accident. It's inevitable.

We've also discovered that gradual random mutations do not account for the big changes. Instead, relatively long stable periods of existence are interrupted by the sudden appearance of dramatically new and higher levels of life. This phenomenon is known as punctuated equilibria or quantum evolution.

Natural selection and survival of the fittest do play a role. But more of an after-the-fact role. Together they go to work on transformations that have already occurred through the big evolutionary leaps; nature's way of finetuning.

Survival of the fittest is a misinterpreted concept.

There is far more cooperation between organisms and environments than competition.

Evolution is man's most important discovery because it's our own creation story.

Still, Darwin heavily influences contemporary thought. Most of us think in terms of competition for survival. "Survival of the fittest" is a deeply ingrained mindset in business, economics, war, love - you name it – it's about competition. You've got to step on a lot of people to get to the top. The strong survive and the weak are eaten. All's fair in love and war. (Insert your cliche here.)

In truth there's much more cooperation between environments and living organisms than was ever imagined by Darwin. Organisms and environments are so inter-related, so connected, they technically co-evolve. As chemist John Lovelock says "so closely coupled is the evolution of living organisms with the evolution of their environments that together they constitute a single evolutionary process."

Competition is not the driving force of evolution we once thought it was and survival of the fittest and natural selection are simply subtexts in a relatively cooperative unfolding of life.

Evolution is by far man's most important discovery. It's our true creation story and we've only begun to fully understand it. Biologically, physically, emotionally, socially, culturally we evolve. It's the only game in town.

Evolve Yourself

Life has a direction

"It is easier to ride a horse in the direction he is going."
— M. Eckhart

"I'm going to catch that horse if I can."
— The Byrds

Okay, so we've accepted the fact that evolution is the general condition of life and that it's inherent in everything. It's not just a theory; it's a fact (even the Pope admits it). Things go along for a while at a certain level then, bang! Suddenly it's on to the next level.

We now understand that evolution is not about competition between organisms and environments, it's about cooperation. This is the essence of the evolution revolution.

Life has an irreversible direction.

*Every single thing has a basic evolutionary impulse
to become more.*

Evolution is a process of transcend and include.

Therefore, we have no choice, we must evolve. Duh!

But there's more. Evolution is a one way street. It has directionality. Everything has a basic drive or impulse to become more. Everything from a rock to human consciousness has a tendency to propel itself into higher more complex levels of organization. As noted author Ken Wilbur puts it, "an amoeba can eventually become an ape, but not vice versa." He describes evolution as a process of "transcend and include."

Simply put, while things evolve to the next higher level (transcend), they still retain the essentials of the lower level (include). Transcend and include. For example, molecules transcend or go beyond atoms, but obviously include atoms. Cells contain molecules and atoms, but they're more than just molecules and atoms. An organism contains cells, molecules and atoms, but is more than just a collection of cells, molecules and atoms — you get the idea. The whole is greater than the sum of its parts. It becomes something new.

Basically, evolution is self-transcendence. Life's direction, simply put, is to become more.

Evolution is the undeniable, irreversible, universal impulse of all things. This direction and the process by which is moves are the keys to understanding where we came from, where we're going and how we're going to get there. It shows us that we really have no choice but to become more than we are. That we have to evolve. And that's good news.

Evolve Yourself

Conscious Evolution

"Human beings now play an active and critical role not only in the process of their own evolution, but in the survival and evolution of all living beings."
— Jonas Salk

"There will be no more biological evolution without conscious evolution."
— Robert Ornstein

So, there you have the basics. The most up-to-date scientific interpretation of the world. The new perspective that's going to have a huge impact on our future. Let's review.

We now see the universe as a dynamic, changing, evolving place and we know that our understanding of it is reflected in every aspect of our lives. We know that everything is connected. Though it may seem like we're separate from the world and each other, we're not. And, finally, evolution is the general condition and everything evolves fol-

---

We're changing the way things change.

We now have the power to alter our own evolution.

This power brings new and profound responsibilities.

The design of evolution is our guide.

---

lowing the same basic pattern of transcend and include in a direction to become more. Whew!

And now we're faced with the very real fact that we have the power to alter our own evolution. We can literally change the way things change.

For instance, we're cloning life; creating it in the laboratory. We're tinkering with DNA and unlocking the mysteries of the brain. We have the power to manipulate our environment; we have the power to destroy it.

In other words, we now have the tools to participate in our own evolution. We have reached a level of technological and scientific sophistication where we're able to effectively control, manipulate and determine our future.

We *will* participate in our own evolution. There is no doubt about that. The question is how? History teaches us that civilizations die from excessive development of the very traits that made them successful in the first place. Which makes us wonder, how will we consciously and conscientiously achieve desirable results for ourselves – both as a society and as individuals?

The answer lies in evolution itself. Duh! The study of evolution is the study of what has worked. The pattern of transcend and include to become greater is a very successful formula. Human consciousness evolves using the same pattern. The psychological, self-help and human potential movements are not narcissistic fads, although to

We are becoming co-creators in our own evolution.

Conscious evolution is the next big leap
in human evolution.

Participating in our own evolution
is part of our evolution.

some they may seem that way. They're actually explorations of and precursors to our inevitable evolutionary leap of consciousness. We *will* surpass and become greater than we are — ethically, morally, spiritually, psychologically and intellectually. And, we'll do it consciously.

In fact, many well-respected scientists and sociologists believe conscious evolution is the next big jump in human development. Conscious evolution recognizes the fact that our merging technologies and hyper sciences not only give us the power to participate in and affect our own evolution, but that that power brings with it new and profound responsibilities. Many believe that with our stunning advances in technology and science, we'd *better* have a leap in human consciousness or the whole thing could blow up in our faces.

This emerging view of ourselves as actively engaging in the process of evolution is actually part of our evolution. So get used to it. For millions of years, humans were at the mercy of the elements. Eventually, we became observers, studying and recording our observations about the world in an effort to understand how the universe works. Within just the last 50 years, we've gone from observer to choreographer. We have become the caretakers of life here on earth, and like it or not, it's time to face the music and learn to dance to it.

Now that we understand the directional nature and

We'll use our new knowledge of the dynamics of evolution to become not only more, but better.

Evolve Yourself

pattern of all of life, we can and must consciously cooperate with evolution to design our future. Evolution is our guide. We can and will combine our new knowledge with a new higher consciousness to become not only more, but better – socially, biologically, culturally, ethically, morally and spiritually.

Evolve Yourself

Reality check

*"We live in a fantasy world of illusion.
The great task is to find reality."*
– Iris Murdoch.

"Reality and perfection are synonymous."
– Spinoza

So, you're thinking, now that I know all this good stuff, what do I do with it? You understand that the one true and real impulse of everything including yourself is to evolve. And that evolution follows a definite pattern to become more. It's undeniable and irreversible.

But now you're asking yourself, how do I align myself with the direction of evolution to further my own personal development? How can I get with the program? Where do I start? Funny you should ask.

Start with where you live. Your mind.

Evolve Yourself

Life is a state of mind

"Whether we are happy depends on inner harmony,
not on the controls we are able to exert over the great forces of the universe."
– Mihaly Csikszentmihalyi

"Most people are about as happy as they make up their minds to be."
– Abraham Lincoln

Your mind plays the most important part in determining the quality of your life. Not your job, your husband or wife, or your kids. Not the "stuff." Your mind.

From studying the brain, we've learned that the mind is not any one thing, but a process working with and through the brain. We receive loads of external information though our senses from countless sources – sights, sounds, touch, smells and tastes. Your mind is the process (your mind doesn't process it, it is the process) that interprets all

---

Your mind plays the most important role in your life.

Your mind is a process; not a "thing."

*Each of us creates our own world
by what we choose to notice.*

Many of our perceptions are in reality conceptions.

this information and converts it into happiness, fulfillment, pain, fear, pleasure, boredom, joy – whatever.

Many of our minds' interpretations happen automatically. Most of the results of our thinking comes from habitually accessing a limited storehouse of already accumulated knowledge, impressions, beliefs, prejudices, memories, wishes and desires that influence our interpretation of the world – interpretations which may or may not be accurate.

To a great extent, our senses are eliminative. We filter out most of the information available to us even before we're aware of it. There's a good reason for this. The flood of information available to our senses at any given moment is not only more than we need to know, it's more than we could endure. So, we unconsciously filter out most of it.

But what sensory information does enters our awareness accounts for a lot less of our perception of world than you may think. Studies have shown, for example, that information relayed from the "external" world through the eye accounts for only 20% of what we use to create a perception. The other 80 percent comes from us. From inside us! From stored knowledge, impressions, beliefs, prejudices, memories, wishes and desires.

Many of your impressions of the outside world, of events, people and relationships are really projections that come from inside you. This means that the quality of your

Life an inside job.

You are your own "world processor".

Consciousness allows us to think about our thinking.

Life is a state of mind.

life is mostly determined by your inner experience; by how and what you think. It means your experience of life isn't overwhelmingly influenced by outside forces. Happiness, contentment, love – all the things we want so badly are *inner* concepts. The quality of your life is an inside job. It's a state of mind.

It's true that we get into ruts of thinking about and interpreting the world. Our lives become monotonous, dreary and unchanging. We shrug and say "that's just the way it is." We placidly accept the hand that life has dealt us, not realizing that for the most part it's really the hand we've dealt ourselves. But it doesn't have to be this way.

It doesn't have to be this way because we've evolved reflective consciousness. Simply put, consciousness is the ability to think about your thinking. Through consciousness, we observe our own mind working and can choose to actively take part in the processing and interpretation of the information we receive. Consciousness allows us to direct and affect our lives; to transcend bad habits of thinking and interpreting.

All you have to do is pay attention to your thinking and actively participate in the process. It's the key to true freedom and control in your life. By rethinking the way you think, you'll break through old limits and go beyond what you were to new levels of understanding. It's what we mean when we say "life is a state of mind."

Evolve Yourself

Beliefs are not facts

"We see what we believe rather than believe what we see."
— Alan Watts

"If what you believe is actually true,
you don't need to believe it."
— Ron Smothermon

What are beliefs really?

Beliefs are opinions, assumptions, prejudices, judgments, ideas and attitudes through which everything you experience in life is filtered.

They're the psychological tools we use to interface with the world; that limited warehouse of stored knowledge we use to analyze, comprehend, categorize and interpret any given situation or event. They are the lenses through which we see the world.

Beliefs label your world.

Most beliefs are inherited.

Beliefs largely determine your experience.

You are fully responsible for your beliefs.

Many of your beliefs were probably inherited from your parents, grandparents, teachers, bosses, spouses – whomever. And you've deduced a bunch of them from books, the media, magazines, movies – whatever. Your beliefs are based on information that was available when you formed them. Some of your beliefs are nearly as old as you. And beliefs you inherited from your parents were probably inherited from their parents, who in turn inherited them from their parents and so on. There's no telling how old some of your beliefs are – beliefs as old as the information they were based on. (We're not talking about tradition here, we are talking about beliefs – we need tradition in our lives.)

Beliefs dictate our experience whether we realize it or not. We automatically notice things we're expecting to see, because we're looking for them. In this way, the world largely conforms to our beliefs about it. The outer world is a reflection of our inner world. If you believe, for instance, that people are inherently bad, then you'll pay more attention to people doing bad things. As you observe life, reality becomes one way – your way. Your observations form a loop and reinforce your beliefs about the world. You'll look at the world and say, "yup, just like I thought!" Beliefs keep you in agreement with yourself.

Maintaining your beliefs feels safe mostly because they're familiar to you. They may feel safe, but in reality,

Beliefs define, but also confine your experience.

Beliefs should be evaluated on how they affect you.

Beliefs are not facts. Beliefs are just beliefs.

beliefs can be dangerous. On the pretense of helping you, they may be severely limiting. Though beliefs are supposed to define your world, they can often confine your world. They narrowly shape what and how you experience life. Sticking stubbornly to your beliefs is not a virtue if they're harming you. It's like driving your car with the brakes on.

Every once in a while you need a belief housecleaning. You need to pull them out, dust them off and take a cold hard look at them. Ask yourself: Are my beliefs still working for me? Are they helping me or hurting me? Common sense dictates we should evaluate our beliefs based on how they affect us and those around us.

Do you really want your mind possessed by static beliefs based on out-of-date or false information? Beliefs that limit your thinking and keep you from expanding your understanding of the ever-changing world around you? Beliefs that keep you from true fulfillment and personal development?

The world is constantly changing. It's a fact. However, to move forward – to evolve – you have to realize that beliefs are not facts. Your beliefs don't even necessarily reflect the truth. In fact, most of the time they don't. You may know what you believe, but believing is not the same as knowing.

But know this: Beliefs are not facts. Beliefs are just beliefs.

Evolve Yourself

Higher consciousness

*"...the tendency toward expanded consciousness and freedom
is the direction of evolution itself."*
– Barbara Marx Hubbard

*"The most exciting breakthroughs of the 21st Century
will not come from advances in technology,
but from what it means to be human."*
– John Naisbitt

You have a choice. You can choose to allow the quality
and direction of your life to be determined unconsciously
by your conditioning and your beliefs, or you can consciously use your understanding of reality.

Choosing the second is the first step toward a new,
higher consciousness and a better, happier, more fulfilling life.

The new higher consciousness is not about shaving
your head, wearing an orange robe or chanting mantras.
It's about consciously expanding your understanding and

Higher consciousness is a perspective
that sees other perspectives.

Higher consciousness is the most practical
approach to life.
It's our greatest advantage.

Higher consciousness
follows evolution's transcend and include pattern,
but it is self-directed.

Evolve Yourself

awareness of what's real in order to make decisions that will produce positive results and make your life work better. The new higher consciousness is about being on the observation deck of your life, so you can see the maze clearly. It's about getting the big picture; about gaining the perspective that sees other perspectives. It's a practical, useful approach to life. With this broader view, you will have more options and more possibilities, and that equals more freedom.

And, you'll be better prepared to deal with the rapid fire rate at which we're pelted with information today. They say the greatest evolutionary advantage of any species is the ability to filter, process and integrate information from its environment. Higher consciousness is our best advantage. Developing an ability to be flexible and view the world through multiple perspectives is how we'll thrive in this new millennium.

Consciousness is at the very core of being human. Developing the new higher consciousness follows the same evolutionary pattern as everything else in the universe. That is to transcend yet include what went before. The big difference between consciousness evolution and cosmic and biological evolution, is that consciousness evolution happens much faster and is self-directed. That means you do it! Awareness and attention are your best tools for raising your consciousness and you don't have to wait millions of years. It unfolds in your lifetime.

*Higher consciousness will change
your relationship to life itself.*

*Higher consciousness is critical
to your personal evolution.*

Still, all real change comes from a change in beliefs. The bottom line is, we all need to filter, synthesize and integrate new information and interpret our old information in new ways. In the process, we'll learn more, broaden our awareness and generate new meaning from every aspect of our lives. We'll become more.

Remember, your outer world reflects your inner world. We can understand only as much of the outer world as we have developed and realized within ourselves. Why strangle your experience of the world by stubbornly sticking to old beliefs and limiting points of view? It might feel safe to you, but you're not evolving. And, when it comes to consciousness you must evolve – yourself. What's the point in living longer if you don't grow?

Evolve Yourself

Science, *Real*igion

"Evolution is simply spirit-in-action."
– Ken Wilber

"God has no religion."
– Gandhi

If you're waiting for science to explain everything, don't hold your breath. Science will never explain everything. And even if it could, science doesn't construe meaning from analysis. Finding meaning is not the mission of science. Finding truth is. Meaning has traditionally been left to religion.

But what is religion anyway? Stripped down, religion is simply a world view. Religions – 100,000 to date – generate meaning and value from an interpretation of existence. Something science, with its analytical eye, hasn't done.

Everybody is looking for a universal explanation.

Science explains the universe with facts.
Religion explains the universe with metaphor.

Science looks for truth.
Religion searches for meaning.

As we said, everybody – especially scientists and theologians – have been looking for the same thing – the big explanation, a unified theory. Science attempts to find it with facts and data; religion with myth and metaphor. Just like us, (because they are us!) each sees only what they want to see.

Religion will never do away with science and our need to know more. In humans, the "why" chromosome is built in. But by the same token, science will never do away with religion because religion is also a function of human nature – man's emotional and psychological need to find meaning. We're predisposed toward religion by that same built-in need to know.

Religion has always played a major cultural role. Early religions helped people cope with their ignorance and fear. Religious rituals gave us confidence, a group identity. Religion was indispensable in times of war as it maintained morale and pulled the community together in the face of the unknown. In other words, religion had survival value.

But today, we are in a totally different position than our ancestors. It wasn't that long ago – several hundred years – that most of the population was illiterate and access to knowledge was extremely limited. But now, through such advancements as personal computers, colleges, universities and public libraries, nearly all of us have access to the accumulated knowledge of mankind, yet our religions have changed precious little. We're living in a society that bene-

Many religious beliefs conflict with scientific fact.

*Science and religion are in agreement:
there is a force in everything.*

We're evolving emotionally, intellectually, morally, ethically...

... why not religiously?

fits from progress created by scientific knowledge, yet many of our religious beliefs are in direct opposition to that knowledge. How weird is that? It's time to rethink our religious beliefs. It's time to put our beliefs in line with what we know. It's time to evolve religiously by extracting meaning from what's real.

Both science and religion agree that there's a force, an intelligence, a spirit in everything. Some call it god; others call it energy. Are they really that radically different? Could evolution be god's way of revealing itself? Could evolution be the universe becoming conscious of itself? We've evolved physically, emotionally, intellectually, morally and ethically. Why not spiritually with a "conscious" religion? A REALigion.

In the new millennium, any belief system or religion must have the capacity to meet, inspire and guide change. Because, as we have seen over and over in this book, change is the only constant. A pregiven never-changing universe is not where we live. It's just the opposite. Evolution is the general condition of all things. (Just ask the Pope.) Our religions and belief systems must use all available knowledge and information to help us understand change and to give us encouragement for the continuing adventure of human development.

Remember, god has no religion, people have religion.

Evolve Yourself

•

Enlightenment

"Understanding others is wisdom.
Understanding yourself is enlightenment."
— Lao Tse

"The secret of enlightenment is to lighten up."
— Unknown

For many of us, the term "enlightenment" conjures up
visions of gurus sitting cross-legged on mountain tops. Of
incense, visions, chants and trances. Of teetering between
the real, perceived world and a mysterious ethereal world.
Of quitting your job, dropping out of society and not wearing shoes.

Never mind all that. Enlightenment is a process just
like anything else. Any experience that expands your consciousness beyond its present limits is enlightening.

The way to become enlightened, is to lighten up.

Enlightenment means letting go of illusions...

...and accepting reality...

... in other words, enlightenment is freedom from always wanting things to be different.

Enlightenment can mean reaching the ultimate state of consciousness – nirvana, satori, bliss – or any point along the way.

So, how do you become "enlightened?" Simple. Just lighten up.

Still, it's easier said than done. You have to dump the excess psychological baggage of defenses, projections, preconceptions, assumptions, prejudices, interpretations, judgments, ideas and attitudes that weigh you down and keep you from seeing the real picture. When you start shedding this unnecessary weight, you become lighter or "enlightened." It's not reality that's bugging you, it's your illusions about reality that are creating the confusion. When you let go of your illusions, you begin to see what's essential in life. All the irritating little superficialities that used to bother you and caused all sorts of complications, don't bother you any more and, what do you know? Life isn't such a problem!

All life is moving in a direction to become more. On a personal level that means self-realization and enlightenment. To become a true human being. It's an impulse we all have. And evolution teaches us that this drive, this desire to become more than what we were before, is built-in. It's inherent in each and every one of us. We can't help it.

Still, we often try to fight it. We cling to old beliefs, we try to deaden the urge with drink or drugs, we muffle it

*Our evolutionary impulse on a spiritual level
is toward enlightenment.*

with poor health, stinkin' thinkin', anger, jealousy, revenge – whatever. Resisting the urge to become better, to become enlightened, makes us sad, mad, unhappy people.

This is why so many people who after reaching all the goals they set for themselves – the big house, the perfect job, the best car, the perfect lawn – still feel unfulfilled. It's because they're ignoring the one built-in goal we all have – enlightenment. But enlightenment is not really a goal in the sense of a destination. It's not something you "get," but something you "discover." Yourself.

Your personal development and quest for enlightenment is the true purpose of your life. It's evolution. And, as you surely must know by now, you have to evolve yourself.

Duh!

Evolve Yourself

Responsibility

*"You are already responsible for your life, totally.
The only question is, 'will you acknowledge that?'"*
— Ron Smothermon

*"Emancipate yourself from mental slavery.
None but ourselves can free our minds."*
— Bob Marley

It takes a lot of courage and integrity to accept responsibility. To rise above our limited perspective and embrace the world as it is requires emotional and intellectual strength. We think we deal in reality all the time, but in truth, it's very hard to see past our illusions.

I hate to say it, but people are like sheep. We like to follow. And we'll follow just about anything. We'll believe in anything except ourselves. We'll believe in organizations that promise eternal life, charismatic people who claim to

We tend to believe in anything but ourselves...

...it relieves us of our responsibility.

But, you are ultimately responsible for your life...

*...which means you owe it to yourself
to find the truth yourself.*

know what god wants, reincarnation and crystals.

Why do we follow? Because it's easier than finding the out the truth for ourselves and creating our own path. It's easier to follow a god or a system of belief or an ideology that purports to give purpose to our lives. Secretly, we all want a father figure to tell us what to do and how to be. It's a responsibility-free existence. "It says so in the Bible." "It's God's way." "I don't make up the rules, lady, I just enforce 'em." "Don't blame me."

Plus, we all have the need to belong to a group. Membership in a group – religion, race, nationality – allows us to be openly righteous and make others wrong if they don't believe, look or live as we do. Individuals in a group are given purpose, confirmation and validation simply through the exclusion of others from that group.

There will always be those of us who would rather believe than know. The fact that man has invented approximately 100,000 religions to date is testimony to our difficulty in getting at the truth. And where has it gotten us? Bound by myth, religion and taboo, man has killed approximately a hundred million of his own kind in the past 60 years alone!

But, the sad fact is, when you put your belief exclusively in a god, ideology or system of thought, to a large extent you give up personal responsibility and lose the experience of choice. Instead of expanding, which is evolution,

Responsibility means "to respond with ability."

Evolve Yourself

you are narrowing, which is regression.

Responsibility literally means "to respond with ability." The only way to do that is to use all of your faculties to investigate the truth for yourself. We're just beginning to open ourselves up to understanding the dynamics of life. There's not just more to learn, but everything to learn. And, it's your personal responsibility to investigate.

Evolve Yourself

?

The meaning of life

"The seeker is always that which is being sought."
— Zen saying

"The meaning of life is whatever you ascribe it to be."
— Joseph Campbell

So, The Big Question. What is the meaning of life? When the Zen student asks the master "Who am I?" The master always answers "Who's asking?"

It's the old answering a question with a question routine. What a gyp.

Or is it?

Maybe, just maybe, the answer really does lie hidden in the question. By turning the question back onto the questioner, the master is encouraging him or her to look to

The search for meaning is the search for self.

The more we evolve our consciousness,
the more meaning is revealed.

themselves for the answer. The master knows it's during this process of searching the magic of self-discovery and self-development happens. Meaning isn't something you get in a book. The master knows the answers are going to come from you. (Duh! That's why he's the master.) Every adventure of self-discovery starts with a question, and the big question "What is the meaning of life" is just a cliche. What the questioner really wants to know is "Who am I and what is my purpose in life?" But as we have seen, a lot of us gravitate toward a final definitive answer from an outside source, a god or a system of belief or an ideology. We look to anything besides ourselves to tell us who we are and what our purpose is. If only it was that easy.

But life doesn't work that way. The name of the game here in this world – the world we live in – is evolution, in other words growth, the process of life itself. It's what this whole book is about! Our only real "job" in life is to evolve. Meaning and purpose emerge as you go through this process. The deeper you get into it, the more meaning is revealed to you. Superficial lives have superficial meanings. The more depth you develop as a person, the more in touch with the "meaning of life" you are. You discover who you are and in this discovery you realize your connection with the "all."

So, is there a meaning to life? Yes. What is it? (Who's asking? Just kidding.) Nobody can answer that for

Only the answers that come from you will have true meaning in your life.

you. If they say they can, run the other way. Because the only way any answer will resonate with you, is if *you* search for it yourself. It's in this process that meaning will emerge. Meaning is a by-product of the searching. It's your life. And, if you take the trouble to explore it authentically, I think you'll be surprised. You'll be getting what you really want instead of what you got talked into.

Evolve Yourself

Evolve yourself

"The best way out is always through."
– Robert Frost

"Live from your own center."
– Joseph Campbell

Our lifetimes are spent searching for the center of the maze – the center of ourselves. Much of that time we spend running frantically around the periphery of self, not realizing that the hedges we can't see over and that keep us hemmed in, are self made. They are constructs of the mind. We're not aware that if we want to get to the center, we have to sometimes question the way the arrows are pointing.

Unfortunately, a lot of what we've been taught by well-meaning parents, teachers and clergy, is not conducive

You have to think for yourself....

*...thinking for yourself and letting go of illusions,
expands your consciousness ...*

*...and ultimately dissolves the maze, allowing you
to live a more balanced life from your center.*

to self-realization. We've been taught how to fit in, get by and do what we're told. That's fine for children. But there comes a time in everyone's life when you have to start thinking for yourself. The inner journey is the only authentic journey precisely because it's *yours*.

All real growth happens on the inside. Each person carries within themselves meaning and purpose. It's only from inner explorations that you uncover meaning and purpose and can fulfill your potential. The maze of your life is self-constructed. You don't have to solve the maze, rather, it dissolves in the basic realization of who you are. When you pay attention to the essentials in life and not the superficialities, then you can find your true center and begin to live from it. And, I guarantee, you'll be happier and more fulfilled.

Consciousness is the uniquely human gift that allows us to get up on the observation deck and see the big picture of our lives. It's from this vantage point that we can clearly see how dynamic and creative our lives can be. By thinking about our thinking, we can see through the illusions and evolve to know the world and ourselves better.

Remember, the universe is a growing, changing and evolving place. Our understanding of it is mirrored in everything we do whether we know it or not. That means, we are growing and changing and, most importantly, evolving. We're evolving just like everything else on earth. People, families, societies, institutions, politics – everything

Evolution is the undeniable, irreversible pattern of all things.

Evolution is the process of transcend and include to become more.

Expanded awareness and higher consciousness are self-directed...

...therefore, to become more, evolve yourself... Duh!

evolves following the same undeniable and irreversible pattern. Including human consciousness. The difference, however, is that human consciousness – your consciousness – is self-directed. In other words, you have to evolve yourself.

By accepting, cooperating with and putting your belief in what's real, you can make an evolutionary consciousness leap and get to the heart of the human experience. As much as we would sometimes like to, we can never return to what was. To paraphrase JFK, we'd like to live as we used to, but history won't let us. The only answer is forward and through.

If you take anything away from this, let it be that evolution equals growth, development and transcendence. Its trajectory – its direction – is always toward higher and higher levels. Apply this undeniable principle to everything in your life, especially your consciousness. Seek the information you need to evolve, to expand your awareness and to grow and develop your consciousness. The self-development experienced through searching for this knowledge allows you to make sense of the universe and your own life and gives you the expansion of meaning and purpose that you're looking for. It doesn't get any better than that!

It's never too late. You can re-choose your approach to living. A shift in consciousness is all it takes. But, nobody can do it for you. The beautiful truth is, you evolve yourself. Duh!

Evolve Yourself

———

"For reality is the goal, deny it how we will.
And we can approach it only
by an ever-expanding consciousness,
by burning more and more brightly,
until memory itself vanishes."

Henry Miller

•

The universe is alive

New information changes our interpretation
of the universe.
We now see the universe as constantly
growing and expanding.
The changing universe is reflected in our
lives.
We live what we know. What we know
changes and therefore we change.

Everything is connected

Science reveals that everything is connected
by an intricate series of relationships –
something we instinctively know.
We're not independent; we're interdependent.
Everything affects everybody.
Our separateness is an optical delusion.

The evolution revolution

Evolution is not a theory or hypothesis. It's a fact.

The appearance of life was not accidental. Life wants to happen.

Life transforms itself to higher levels by jumps or leaps, not by a gradual "piling on" of mutations.

There is far more cooperation between organisms and environments than competition.

Evolution is man's most important discovery because it's our creation story.

Life has a direction

Life has an irreversible direction.

Evolution is a process of transcend and include.

Everything has a basic evolutionary impulse to become more.

We have no choice but to evolve.

Conscious evolution

We are changing the way things change.
We now have the power to alter our own
    evolution.
This power brings new and profound
    responsibilities.
The design of evolution is our guide.
Conscious evolution is the next big leap in
    human evolution.
Participating in our own evolution is part of
    our evolution.

Life is a state of mind

Your mind plays the most important role in
    your life.
Your mind is a process; not a "thing".
Each of us creates our own world by what
    we choose to notice.
Many of our perceptions are in reality
    conceptions.
You are your own "world processor".

Beliefs are not facts

Beliefs label your world.
Your experience is largely determined by
your beliefs.
They define but also confine your
experience.
Beliefs should be evaluated on how they
affect you.
You are fully responsible for your beliefs.
Beliefs are not facts. They are beliefs.

Higher consciousness

Higher consciousness is a perspective
that sees other perspectives.
Developing higher consciousness is the
most practical approach to life.
Higher consciousness follows evolution's
transcend and include pattern,
but it's self-directed.
Higher consciousness is critical to your
personal evolution.

Science, *Real*igion

Science explains the universe with facts.
Religion explains the universe with metaphor.
Science looks for truth.
Religion searches for meaning.
Science calls it evolution.
Religion calls it God.
Science and religion are in agreement:
    there's a force in everything.

● Enlightenment

The way to become enlightened, is to let go
    of your illusions about reality.
Enlightenment is freedom from always
    wanting things to be different.
Our evolutionary impulse on a spiritual level
    is toward enlightenment.

Responsibility

We tend to believe in anything but ourselves – it relieves us of responsibility.
But, you are ultimately responsible for
your life.
You owe it to yourself to find the truth
yourself.
Responsibility means "to respond with
ability".

The meaning of life

You must answer the meaning question
in your life.
The search for meaning is the search
for self.
The more we evolve personally,
the more meaning is revealed to us.

Evolve yourself

Evolution is the undeniable, irreversible
force in all things.
Evolution is the process of transcend
and include to become more.
Consciousness evolves by the same
process, but is self-directed.
Therefore, to become more, you evolve
yourself. Duh!

Evolve Yourself

Bibliography

Ash, Mel. Shaving the Inside of your Skull: Crazy wisdom for discovering who you really are. New York, Putnam, 1996.

Barlow, Connie,ed. Evolution Extended: Biological Debates on the Meaning of Life. Massachusetts: MIT , 1994.

Campbell, Joseph. The Hero with a Thousand Faces. New Jersey: Princeton University Press, 1949.

Capra, Fritjof. The Web of Life. New York: Anchor, 1996.

Csikszentmihalyi, Mihaly. Flow. New York: Harper and Row, 1990.

Ferguson, Marilyn. The Aquarian Conspiracy. California: J. P. Tarcher, 1980.

Goleman, Daniel. Vital Lies, Simple Truths. New York: Simon and Schuster, 1985.

Hubbard, Barbara Marx. Conscious Evolution: Awakening the Power of Our Social Potential. California: New World Library, 1998.

Johnson, Robert. Transformation: Understanding the three levels of masculine consciousness. New York: Harper Collins, 1991.

Miller, Henry. The Wisdom of the Heart. New York: New Directions, 1941.

Miller, Henry. Stand Still Like the Hummingbird. New York: New Directions, 1962.

Mitchell, Stephen, ed. The Enlightened Mind: An Anthology

Evolve Yourself

of Sacred Prose. New York: HarperCollins, 1991.

Murphy, Michael. Golf in the Kingdom. New York: Penguin, 1972.

Nisker, Wes. Crazy Wisdom. California: Ten Speed, 1990.

Ornstein, Robert E. The Evolution of Consciousness: The Origins of the Way We Think. New York: Touchstone, 1991.

Smothermon, Ron. Winning Through Enlightenment. California: Contex Publications, 1997.

Schumacher, E.F. A Guide for the Perplexed. New York: Harper and Row, 1977.

Wheatley, Margaret J, and Myron Kellner-Rogers. A Simpler Way. California: Berret -Koehler, 1996.

Wiber, Ken. A Brief History of Everything. Boston: Shambhala, 1996.

Wilber, Ken. The Marriage of Sense and Soul: Integrating science and religion. New York: Random House, 1998.

Zirker, Lorette. ed. Finding a Way: Essays on spiritual practice. Boston, Mass: Tuttle, 1996.

Rich Rahn

By the time he was 10, Rich Rahn had been in each of the 48 contiguous states, Mexico, Canada and England, learning more about the world through experience than through the classroom. Not surprisingly, when he was expelled from his Michigan high school at age 17, he headed out alone for the surfing life in California. At 19, he found himself caught up in one of the most notorious drug busts of the century, learning several harsh life lessons. Given probation instead of prison, Rich was off to college, marriage and fatherhood in Ohio where he published a successful series of joke books. Still, he instinctively knew there was more to life. Rich's personal search for meaning took him to Spain, Florida, Cape Hatteras, back to California, a thousand miles off the coast of Mexico on a tuna boat, through hundreds of books and eventually home to Michigan. But his real journey was his inner search. In *Evolve yourself*, Rich introduces the reader to what he's discovered about life and the pursuit of happiness.